Our Father

Published by
Words from God,
17 Orient Street,
Batemans Bay, NSW 2536, Australia.
Telephone:
National (044) 72 9559
International +61 44 72 9559
Facsimile:
National (044) 72 6749
International +61 44 72 6749

© Matthew Kelly, 1995
ISBN 0 646 22913 3

Books available from:

Australia	United States of America
Words from God,	The 101 Foundation,
17 Orient St, Batemans Bay,	P.O. Box 151, Asbury
NSW 2536	New Jersey 08802-0151
Telephone: (044) 72 9559	Telephone: (908) 689 8792
Fax: (044) 72 6749	Fax: (908) 689 1957
United Kingdom	Ireland
2 Barling Road	66 Landscape Park
Great Wakering	Churchtown
Essex SS3 0QB	Dublin 14
Telephone: (0702) 582 335	Telephone & Fax:
	01-298 5403
	01-628 7348

Typeset by Chain Bay Graphics

Foreword

Many people will take up this book and read it from cover to cover and have a warm feeling in their hearts, perhaps momentarily their hearts will even be moved in a strong and profound way. This feeling would be similar to the feeling a boy would have, if for many years he had never known his father, except by what others had said about him, until one day when all of a sudden his father appeared on his doorstep, spent a few hours with the boy and then disappeared again.

In that brief meeting it wouldn't matter how much love that man showed his son because in only a short time that love would be a fading memory, growing forever distant, because love needs to be renewed each day.

The love of Our Heavenly Father is very different from this brief meeting of father and son. It should be something that is alive and present in our everyday lives, unfortunately for many it is not.

I have not selected these excerpts from the hundreds of pages of messages I have received over the past eighteen months because they are entertaining or controversial, nor because they provide something to add to the collection of Heavenly material that these times are providing. No, "Happy the man who is instructed by Truth itself, not by signs and passing words." Rather, I have chosen them because they have helped me to come to know the gentle, warm and deep love of Our Heavenly Father. They have led me to His

Son Jesus Christ and my belief is that they will help others do the same.

There is only one God and He is the God of all men and all women. In this collection of messages I have tried to select messages that allow all persons capable of seeing God as their Father, to grow in understanding His paternal care for each one of us.

Each message bears a truth of love, the truth of God's love. Open the book, read a message and allow your Heavenly Father to speak to you, to guide you, to encourage you, to love you, to direct you, to correct you, to laugh with you, to cry with you, to comfort you, to walk with you, and to live with and in you.

Find the truth in each message and then invite that truth to come and live in you. Reflect slowly on each message and ponder your life in conversation with your loving Father and His Son Jesus Christ. Allow your heart and mind to open and your life to change gracefully bringing forth the joy, that is the Christian life, and making you free.

What is before you is a set of spiritual considerations that embody the love of Our Heavenly Father and the truth of the gospel message. How great they are is irrelevant unless you, as an individual, are prepared to take them into the classroom of prayer with the great teacher, silence. And if you consider the content of these messages calmly, slowly and often, then you will begin to feel the love of a Father who has walked every step of your life with you.

And then your relationship with God will change and it is only a logical consequence that such would transform the words and actions of your life. From that moment on your recollection of God the Father will not be a fading memory of a moment in which you felt His love; nor will you hold the image of an old grey haired man with a long white beard, sitting on a rocking chair wielding His justice with an iron rod; His love won't be something of which you are uncertain and hope to discover in the next life; far from all of this, the love of the Heavenly Father will be the comfort of your life.

May you hear the voice of your Father in Heaven in the lines of this book encouraging you to live the Christian life.

Matthew Kelly
Sunday 2nd October, 1994.
Feast of the Guardian Angels
New Jersey, U.S.A.

1

Strength of character comes from prayer.

2

When it all comes down to it, what you have done for Me is all that counts.

3

When the people around you are weak, you must be strong.

4

You should love all. Those who don't love you in return will be overcome, their hearts will be softened and in the Spirit of My Son Jesus, you will win their hearts.

5

Don't worry about what lies far in front of you. Deal with the task I have given you for this moment.

6

My child, I have built a fire in your heart. Prayer, the Mass and the rosary are the logs on the fire and are what will keep the fire burning strong.

7

The Love of your Father is greater than any force on earth, so just trust in Me.

8

Peace My son. Peace of mind, peace of heart, peace of soul. My Peace.

9

What is gained quickly is lost quickly.

10

My gifts are plentiful to those that open themselves to them.

11

By disciplining yourself to work well, you will gain enormous inner strength which will allow you to love Me better in everything else you do.

12

Smile, say less and listen more, pray and trust in Me, your Heavenly Father.

13

Express your love for Me in the way you treat other people and in the work that you do.

14

What you hope and dream for is small, compared to what I have planned for you.

15

I sent My Son to save the world. Throughout the ages I have had to rely on few to carry His message, light and love. I ask you to carry His message wherever you go. Make His love the centre of all your relations with people. Make His light shine from you. Let His love find a way into every corner of your body.

16

Don't divide your heart, give it all to Me and there will be room for all.

17

Be sure to guard against the wickedness and snares of the devil who will try to make you believe that to be idle is desirable or deserved.

18

Do your work well, down to the last detail.

19

Simplicity is the key to living the life I want you to live.

20

Your time is a great gift from Me your Father, but a limited one. Use it well.

21

The love of your Heavenly Father is warm, affectionate and consistent.
Human love on the other hand is inconsistent and that is why I must be united in, and indeed the centre of, all human love. It is by this, that human love gains consistency and strength in difficult times. It is by this, that human love is sanctified.

22

What good is an earthly love, if it costs you your inheritance to heaven?

23

Look at yourself openly and honestly with humility and realise your human weaknesses.
Then bring them to Me, your Heavenly Father, for I make the weak strong.

24

You must not become a slave to your body. You must condition it so it becomes a suitable home for Me to live in, a suitable instrument for Me to use.

Mortification and penance are useful forms of disciplining and should be exercised daily, even if only in little ways, to condition the body.

25
You are a physical and spiritual being. Your physical state is temporal; your spiritual state is eternal. That which lasts forever should reign over that which is temporal. The spirit should lead the body; the body should not lead the spirit.

26
Be gentle when you speak because you can cause much damage with your words.

27
The lost sheep will return by friendship.

28
Prayer strengthens and gives true authenticity to any gift.

29
There must be a sense of urgency about My work but you should never lose your peace and calm.

30
It is when times are tough that you show Me that you really love Me.

31

All will be provided.

32

I only ask that you struggle. So struggle with all your might.

33

Think at the end of each day, who did I treat the worst today? And that is how you have treated Me.

34

People are precious; each one deserves your undivided attention when you are with them.

35

Never be content.

36

If you look at children and spend time with them, you will learn many things.

37

Children are a fountain of supernatural direction; be with them.

38

Trust.

39

The light will be shed step by step, the doors opened one by one.

40

Ask yourself: Does this person aspire to live the kind of life I'm trying to live?

After you have answered these questions you will know what is in your midst.

41

Ask and you shall receive.

42

The people who come into your life are all important and all need your encouragement and help, either by prayer or a few gentle words.

43

When you speak about supernatural matters, don't be like those who go on for hours. Be short. Say briefly and simply what it is the Spirit is prompting you to say, and no more.

44

Those who share your love for Me sometimes
need reminding of their duty to spread the faith.
Example is the best reminder.

45

That person next to you on the train or in front of
you on the footpath, that person has a soul. Pray.

46

Try. This one word sums up all I ask of you.

47

You can only fail if you don't try.

48

In times of physical illness remember the joy of
knowing Me. I don't abandon you in sickness, I am
always with you.
Your illness is all that you have to offer Me for
your sanctification on some days.

49

The time is right now for many things.

50

You are called to live as the first Christians did.
Looking out for each other, loving and caring
selflessly for the community.

51

You have nothing to fear My sons and daughters, each one of you must do your own little bit. It may seem insignificant, but little by little we will win. Evil cannot reign over good, evil cannot victor over good, you must trust in Me and do as I ask courageously.

52

If you compromise on the Catholic principles of life, which are elementary, then there is no doubt any faith that remains will be weak and waiver in the wind.

53

Are you serious about living the way I want you to live? Then you must realise the importance of the cross.

54

Ask yourself many times a day: What would Christ do now?

55

Faith sustains joy.

56

Time is short.

57

My plan for each of My children is beautiful. Does a father on the earth plan good and beautiful things for his children? Well, won't My plan from Heaven be of much greater beauty?

58

Fight My child, against those inclinations that lead you to be easy and weak on yourself, or to neglect your duties.

59

Fasting saves souls.

60

If you knew just how powerful prayer was, you would never lose your attention in Mass.

61

My angel will go before you and prepare your way, if you ask him to.

62

Your guardian angel is more beautiful and caring and watchful than anyone you know on earth.

63

Demand what is good and proper and pleasing to God. Demand respect, in particular for your bodies. Dress modestly and properly. Be prudent.

64

Little things are beautiful, big things are necessary.

65

Admit your littleness.

66

Don't compromise your love for Me.

67

Love is selfless.

68

Carry the cross and you will know the unshakeable joy that this brings. Then your life will take on a whole new direction.

69

Adopt the one Holy and Catholic ambition and goal: to do God's will.

70

Don't be alarmed by change.

71

Do you not see that what is before you is all temporary, but what I offer is eternal, eternal joy and happiness?

72

The cross is what gives Christian hearts firmness. Firmness to remain in My love at times of trial, when it costs; the firmness required to be selfless.

73

Give Me your heart and I will make it gentle and kind. Give Me your mind and I will make it strong and wise. Give Me your body and I will make it a useful instrument. Give Me your soul and I will make it My home.

74

Pride stunts your growth.

75

You are fast to react to other people's failings and flaws, but slow to investigate your own. Examine yourself honestly, make one firm resolution and then go off again and put it into practice.

76

Pride separates man from God.

77

You must be cheerful, because holiness and cheerfulness are synonymous. Do you expect to attract people to Christ if you are always unhappy?

78

If you can be the best, you have no excuse for not being the best.

79

Each hour ask yourself: Is this hour a suitable gift to God? Then try harder in the next hour to please Me.

80

Today you must learn to live with Me each moment. One at a time, you and I will tackle the moments that make up the day.

81

Be patient.

82

Every person is different and precious. Until you start to treat them like this you will never be able to do My work effectively.

83

Is it too much to deny your body constantly of the luxuries that make your body lazy and prevent you from being a good instrument of My work?

84

Be brave and fearless. Tirelessly set about doing My work because so many are working so hard against Me.

85

Keep in touch with what is happening in the world.

86

Avoid the fruitless exercises that the world provides 24 hours a day.

87

Television is the thief of love.

88

Be like the blind man. Each day you should cry, 'Lord, open My eyes.'

89

Don't say, 'When this is over I'll devote myself to God.' Give yourself to Me now, completely, once and for all.

90

Worry is a disease and it attacks the beautiful virtue of hope.

91

Worry is useless. By worrying you deny that Divine Providence exists and you deny the gift of hope that I have given to each of My children.

92

My children, if you don't go to confession you tie My hands with the perfection of My justice, but more than this, you deny yourselves one of the greatest gifts I have given you through My Son Jesus.

93

When you are with people, you must give yourself to them for that moment. If you give them only half your attention, you give Me only half your attention.

94

Tomorrow does not belong to you yet.

95

Never cause an argument that can be avoided, and it can be avoided if there is not a moral issue involved.

96

Now is the time, you are the person, and change is the need.

97

On special feast days celebrate in your homes.

98

At work have a small crucifix on your desk.

99

Avoid gossip. Is it that hard to change the topic?

100

Control your imagination.

101

From anything that is bad, I extract good.

102

Don't worry My children, like a father cuddles his children in the night when a thunder storm is raging, so will I cuddle you in My love.

103

Christ is your example My children.

104

Most of you are called to live as Jesus did for the first thirty years of His life.

105

You say you don't have time: make time and I will multiply the effectiveness of all your other work.

106

So many of you search for life in this world, but in the wrong places. Many of you grow old, and still your hunger is not quenched and you wonder why not. It is because I am life, and the way you come to Me is through My Son Jesus Christ. The life you are looking for is in the Blessed Eucharist.

107

My children, you are body and soul and you have a duty to feed both.

108

Join nations at the seams with Christ's love.

109

The cross is large and heavy, cold and harsh, but the fruits of the cross are eternal.

110

Each soul deserves individual attention.

111

The harvest is great but the labourers are few. Go and work in My fields.

112

What is God's will for me now? Ask yourself this often throughout the day.

113

I your Heavenly Father will always give you the graces necessary to carry out My will.

114

Keep your heart under lock and chain in case you become attached to something of this world not intended for you.

115

If you are to sustain the truths of the Catholic Church through these times, you must know them. You must read and study.

116

Do you know the commandments?

117
Take Christ into your workplace.

118
Take yourself away from those earthly attachments and you will discover the real beauty of your faith. You will grasp Catholic doctrine and take it to heart and make a home in your heart for it.

119
Become docile to the promptings of the Holy Spirit.

120
I am the Lord your God, I have a beautiful plan for the world and for each individual. Trust in Me, I know what is most beneficial for your soul, child.

121
Pray for your family.

122
Charity is a selfless stand, often hidden, for the benefit of another person or people.

123
Your mere presence should be enough to signal that certain types of behaviour and conversations are not acceptable.

124

Does your outward conduct reflect the existence
of My Word in your heart?

125

You all have a duty to spread the faith.

126

Be warm, be understanding, be gentle, be humble,
be prudent, be calm, and remember no one can
harm your soul.

127

Be modest in appearance and in the way you act.

128

Be master of your body.

129

Don't over eat or over drink. Gluttony is a
forerunner for impurity.

130

The greatest reward in Heaven is given to the
obedient.

131

If any of your apostolic activity is to be fruitful, it
will be an overflow of your interior life.

132

Get out of bed at a fixed time. Set a fixed time for your prayer. Set a fixed time to retire in the evenings.

133

Your time and energy should be devoted to proclaiming the truth.

134

If you want to be perfect you must be simple. Perfection is found in simplicity.

135

By doing something poorly you will never perfect it.

136

A good child is cheerfully obedient.

137

If you only knew the delight I take in My saints - just men in the middle of the world. You should never underestimate the lengths I will go to, to help one such man.

138

Don't despise the world for I, your Heavenly Father, made it.

139

It is up to you to work in My fields and My fields
are the streets and alleys of your lives.

140

Do not give anyone reason to count you as an
enemy.

141

You must carry the cross in the area of friendship;
many will not understand. They will say you are
not the person you once were. Fear not, follow
firmly along your way; the way that you know is
right. The reason they don't recognise you is
because it is no longer you who lives, but Christ
who lives in you.

142

Go today and sit in front of a tabernacle and speak
to My Son Jesus. Tell Him about all your worries
and fears and He will remove all your anxieties.
Tell Him about your plans for the day and the joys
and problems you expect to encounter. Too many
of you only tell Us of problems. Many beautiful
things are happening, share them with Us in
prayer. Speak to Us about everything that is
happening in your lives. As your Friends, We
want to know.

143

It is in My plan for you that you find the only real happiness on this earth.

144

The greatest dignity that I can bestow on a man is to be a priest.

145

Give everything to Me and then you will be truly happy. Give until you are empty and then I will be your fill.

146

Ask yourself: What am I holding back from God? How can I love God more?

147

At Baptism, apart from sanctifying grace, you receive a mission. That mission is to spread the faith.

148

The beauty of Catholicism is every human being's right.

149

Forgiveness comes from Heaven.

150

Day in day out the same things, and you tell Me that it all becomes so monotonous and that you feel tied down. The problem is you have little love.

151

Pray everyday.

152

Think, occasionally when things go well, or something goes badly, that somewhere in the world Mass is being said, and you are receiving the fruits and graces of that Mass.

153

Pride is the enemy of trust.

154

Sacrifice is often the most heartfelt prayer.

155

Don't limit Me, your God, to the scope of your intelligence.

156

Go to confession regularly.

157

Pray for your friends.

158

You must show concern for every soul. Out of one hundred souls, you are interested in one hundred.

159

Personal sanctification is the only preparation for the times that await at the doorstep of the world.

160

A new day. Each day is a new day, My children. Two are never the same. Today I will present you with many different opportunities to love Me. Each day new and exciting ways of loving Me. Each task you do, each worry you have, every person that enters your life is an opportunity to love. Don't waste these opportunities that I lay in your path to love Me.

Be humble and submit to My will, that is the greatest love you can show Me.

161

Prayer first then sacrifice; these will prepare your heart. Then act from your heart and speak from the overflow of your interior life.

162

Keep calm and happy and let Me do the rest, My children.

163

My child, you must renew your commitment at every moment of the day to remain a faithful instrument. A paint brush that no longer paints well is tossed away by an artist.

164

Place your trust in Me. I will be the wisdom within you and I will be the truth you proclaim. Open your heart repeatedly and abandon your plans and adopt only Mine.

165

Study, so you can defend the faith.

166

How many of My children come to Me begging for a partner in marriage.

My children, marriage is a vocation. Firstly you are all called to the general Christian vocation, then some are called to be priests and religious, others to be married, and some to lead single lay lives. One is not better than the other. All you must do is discover which one I ask of you. It is then, and only then, that you will find true happiness.

You ask for happiness: search for your vocation and you will find happiness. You forget that your vocation is a Divine plan, and there is no better plan than that.

Pray My children, that your eyes might be opened to your vocation and then if you feel you are called to marriage, pray for a Holy Catholic marriage and partner.

Seek first the kingdom of God and all else will be given to you in addition.

Marriage is not for everyone. Society paints a sad picture of religious life, as it does of priestly life, because people have forgotten that regardless of their calling, they must sacrifice. Sacrifice is called for by Me, your Heavenly Father from all of you.

My children, you must seek to deny yourself in everything you do. First see that whatever state of life you are called to, will involve many great sacrifices and uncomfortable little sacrifices. Then you will be ready to respond to My call with love.

Don't be selfish, because in the end you will see that this life is not to be one of pleasure, but sacrifice and pain.

167

My children, come to Me in your hour of need and lay your request on My Heavenly altar with prayer from the depths of your heart, in My Son Jesus Christ's name; but always submit to My will.

168

Pray and a new world will be opened to your eyes.

169

Today My children, look to your Mother Mary. Consider how many times in the Litany you have cried, "Cause of our joy," and why is she the cause of your joy? Because she has brought Christ to all men.

When Mary visited Elizabeth, she brought joy to Elizabeth's household because she brought Christ.

My children, get to know Christ My Son, as the companion that accompanies you along the roads of your lives, because it is then that you will start to bring joy to people, because you bring to them Christ.

170
Love is everyday.

171
Give generously and with a warm heart. Give until it hurts in everything. And most importantly, give with a smile on your lips and a song in your heart, because I love cheerful givers.

172
Follow My Son's path earnestly My children. Don't listen to the dogs as they bark of slander while you walk past. Listen to those who truly know Me and they will whisper, 'Christ is passing by.'

173
Study your faith. Then live your faith. Then and only then will you be able to spread the Catholic truths.

174
Don't get caught up in a hundred books.

175
With Me you lack nothing.

176

Examine your intention. If it is to do the will of God, then turn your cheek to those who persecute you. The suffering that you are put through should be offered to Me, your loving Father, for the benefit of those souls who persecute you.

177

My children, I give you My Mother for she will make all your works fruitful. Send all your words and actions through her Immaculate Heart.

178

Wherever you go, whatever you do, sow the seeds of My love, My children.

179

A flame that shudders on a still night is a proud flame. The movement in the flame is not caused by the wind, but comes from the lack of harmony within.

My child, you are My light to the world in these times, you must shine brightly and consistently. Don't let any wind or dampness put you out. I am the flame that burns within you and I will never leave you.

Beware of pride My child, this is how the devil will try to tempt you. Remember always that you are just an instrument. My child, only you and your pride will put out the beautiful flame I have lit in your heart.

Struggle always to be humble and prudent, for you are the light I want to set on a hill.

180

Teach people to be humble by your example of humility.

181

A proud soul is content with ignorance.

182

Make your heart firm but gentle, loving and full of compassion. It is from your heart that all your actions and words come.

183

Show Me that your prayer life isn't just because it gives you good feelings.

184

Order is the virtue of the humble.

185

My child, the way you must travel is narrow and hard. At times you will feel that there is no one with you, but I am always with you.

186

Just let Christ increase in you, open your heart, and long and hunger for My will, and all will be well.

187

Ask yourself: Did I speak out of concern for souls in all my words, or did I speak for self gratification, to be noticed, or some other selfish motive?

188

Were my good works and my sacrificing kept as hidden as they could be, so that my love of God was not endangered by earthly applause?

189

Do I seek always to tell the truth even when people's higher opinion of me will be damaged? Do I recognise that of my own I am nothing, and that it is only because of the grace of God that I have all of my abilities? Am I grateful to God for all He has given me or am I always wanting for more?

190

In my study of the faith, do I seek knowledge so as only to repeat it like a parrot, or in my knowledge seeking, do I make a sincere attempt to place those words in my heart and then live them?

191

Listen more and say less.

192

Change.

193

My children, you need a change of heart. Follow Jesus for He is meek and humble of heart.

194

Obedience is for the humble.

195

All the answers are in the tabernacle. And so all the answers will come from the tabernacle. My children, Christ's body, blood, soul and divinity are in the tabernacle. When you put Christ in your hearts then you will have the answers.

And how do you put Christ in your hearts? Prayer, sacrifice and the sacraments. Spend time each day in front of the tabernacle. Spend yourself each day in mortification. And frequent the sacraments.

My children, for ages you have known that Christ is the way, the truth and the life, now you must act on this knowledge. Invite the Holy Spirit into your lives today and He will teach you how to let God reign in your hearts. Then He will teach you how to discern these answers.

196

People are precious.

197

Face up to the real person that you are.

198

It is clear that you want to love Me My children, but so often you find yourselves held to ransom by worry and anxiety. My children, the answer is in consistent love of Me.

199

The struggle is long and hard but the road leads to Heaven.

200

You have learnt that the only way to Heaven is through Jesus My Son and that this path is inseparable with the cross.

201

One day at a time.

202

Some days will be long and hard, others will seem short and easy. You must learn to love Me on both of these days.

203

Order is a virtue of the humble; could it be that you are still so proud that you don't see the need for it?

204

A proud soul doesn't need to be tempted by sin.

205

Be witnesses to Christ.

206

After prayer share your knowledge with those around you. Friendship is the secret.

207

Come My children, gather around the tabernacle where My Son Jesus lives and remember that those who have seen the Son have seen the Father, so those who are near the Son are near the Father and where the Father is, so is the Son.

Children you don't understand what a privilege it is to have so many churches, in your area, in your country, in the world, that have My Son's precious body and blood present in them. Yet so many of you pass by churches indifferent to His presence.

Today My children, I invite you to an intimate relationship with My Son Jesus. A friendship that holds nothing back but shares everything in truth and honesty. The friend, the companion that all of you have sought in your lives is in the tabernacle. The friend who is so dedicated to His friendship, yet so unappreciated.

Start to spend time daily in front of the tabernacle and talk to Jesus as you would the best of friends. Tell Him of your worries and joy. Ask Him how you can help your friends. Ask Him to ask Me, your Heavenly Father, to send the Holy Spirit upon you, and I will.

Open your eyes and you will see the greatest friend of your lifetime before you in the tabernacle.

Now you know, you need to foster a friendship, and remember, friendships can be hard sometimes, especially at first.

208

You are all just children in My eyes.

209

Follow the light, live in the light; My children you must follow My Son Jesus Christ. Read about His life on earth daily, just for a few minutes.

210

Don't live by feelings.

211

If you grow to know the Holy Spirit you will hear His call to goodness and then He will lead you in the fulfilment of My will.

212

In each moment of each day you must have Christ at the pinnacle of your lives.

213

You must work to better yourself. Perfect the human elements, by discipline, examination and prayer, because it is upon these that I will build.

214

You all must learn to find comfort in the truth, and
that truth is: Christ will reign.

215

These times are harsh and so the only answer is
saints! Saints greater than those of any age. Saints
more determined than ever to see the will of God
done on earth as it is in Heaven. Saints who want
for nothing else but My will. Holy men and
women prepared to sacrifice everything of a
temporal nature to see My most Holy Will done.

216

Sacrifice constantly to allow your souls to breathe,
to stop your souls from drowning in the waters of
impulse.

217

Give back to Me what is Mine, everything.

218

Stop wasting time.

219

The answers, I tell you, are in the tabernacle, but
only today's answers, and tomorrow's answers will
be there tomorrow.

220

My children, as your Heavenly Father, could you expect Me to have anything but the best of plans for you? However, My plans are Divine plans and sometimes you will just have to accept them. Then days, weeks, or years down the track you will look back and think of the events that you couldn't reason with and see the Divine beauty of My plans for you.

221

Visit My Son Jesus daily in the tabernacle, foster this friendship and He will share with you the answers. From the tabernacle Jesus will lay to rest all your anxieties and worries, He will show you how to live in the peace and joy of love.

222

Happy people are the wealthiest people in the world.

223

Let people see the happiness you have inside you.

224

Smile. The gift of a smile can make a person's day.

225

Amongst the complexity of the world today you must all search for simplicity, My children.

Simplicity is the key to perfection. You must all seek perfection. Seek to be perfect for your Heavenly Father is perfect.

In Christ My children, you have perfection, perfect man and perfect God. Look and learn, listen and hear, for Jesus Christ is the lamb of God who takes away the sins of the world and happy are those who hear the gentle hum of His call.

226

Stop waiting for Me to speak to you through your ears. Open your hearts and your minds to My voice and you will hear My call many times a day.

227

Spend some time in silence, listening to the gentle flutterings I will create in your heart.

228

Meditate on the most perfect sacrifice of My Son Jesus. Spend time reflecting on His passion and death, and the whole meaning of pain will change in your life.

229

You have a headache; what comparison is that to being scourged at the pillar? Offer it up and move on and do your daily duties.

230

Great saints are formed over time, but in every moment.

231

Remember you are dust and unto dust you shall return.

232

They can harm your body, but they cannot touch your soul. Your soul is inseparable from My love, unless you consent to such separation.

233

Victory is assured. Persevere.

234

Even the most menial task, if done well, is valuable in the process of your sanctification if it is done for Me.

235

When it all comes down to it, all that counts is what you have done for Me.

236

Do you not see that you must do everything,
everyday, with a higher meaning.

237

Some steps are large, and some steps are small.
Some steps are hard and some steps are easy, but
all must be taken.

One step at a time My child, no need to rush
anything. Everything is taken care of and it will all
seem to happen too quickly anyway, but fear not,
everything is planned.

You must fight discouragement and put order in
your life to avoid unnatural tiredness. Order will
give you strength.

My child, I am with you.

238

I sent My Son Jesus to show you the way. Speak
as He spoke.

239

In the light of criticism remain silent. Silence has
a strength.

240

Ask yourself: When was the last time I laid my
head on my pillow of an evening, knowing I had
done all that I could?

241

Rebuild My Church. The job is not easy, but like any building one brick is placed at a time and the more bricklayers you have the faster the building is built.

242

Pray each day to the Holy Spirit.

243

Frequent the Blessed Eucharist, receive the precious bread of life as often as possible.

244

If you don't pray then you neglect Me no matter how many charitable works you do. For prayer gives value and meaning to all your work.

245

Do not be as foolish as to think that because what you have to carry out is a Divine plan that you will not encounter any opposition. It is more for that reason than any other, that you will encounter opposition.

246

In the day to day happenings of your everyday life are hidden new and exciting ways of loving Me.

247

Do you not see that this life can fade in an instant?

248

The gods of this world only bring you emptiness. Come to Me for I will be your fill in this life and the life to come.

249

My dear children, foster more friendships for it is in friendships that the seed of conversion is sown.

250

One friend. If all those souls thirsting for the Truth only had one good Catholic friend!

251

At times you will come across souls that are too cowardly to face themselves, pray for them. Hearts change. Cold hearts can be warmed by the love of Christ.

252

Read the Bible. Say the rosary. Go to confession.

253

Make an examination of conscience everyday.

254

My dear children, some days seem like they will never end and some days fly by with the wind. It is precisely for this reason that you need to establish a few set ways of expressing your love for Me.

It is these things that, on those long days, will keep you from becoming discouraged and encourage you to move on with the fire of My love alive within you.

And it is these things that will allow you to keep Me at the centre of your lives when things are all going well and fast. Your lives must be centred around your God, and I am the Lord your God.

255

Look at those around you, look at yourself My child, do you not see that when you let Me be your all that you are happy.

Today My child, reflect on whether your life revolves around Me or whether you just fit Me in if or when you can.

How important am I in your individual happenings of each day? Do you often recognise My presence throughout the day? Do you try to remember My presence in everything you do? Or do you ignore Me except during your time of prayer?

Make a fixed time today for prayer with My Son in the tabernacle. Make a fixed time for each day and then stick to it. By doing this your lives will begin to be centred around Me, the Lord your God.

256

My children, now is your time, don't waste it. If you cannot learn to make use of this very moment to love and serve Me, then the devil will distract you from your aim in the next as well.

My children, you must remember that the devil is active in many ways in the world around you and manifests his hatred under many masks.

You must love My children, for love will crush him. Ask your mother Mary to lend you her heart, so that you can love in the way she loves, free of corruption. If you love all people and seek constantly to fulfil My will, then all will be well.

My plan is the most glorious plan, so please respond to My loving warnings and appeals.

257

A little here and a little there. If you sow the seed of My love like this, you will surely gather a great harvest.

258

To give your life for one soul would be a more than worthy cause. Now do you see that you can never pray enough for one soul?

259

There is no easy way to Heaven.

260

I am a kind and compassionate God, but I am a just God. In fact I am perfectly kind and compassionate, but My perfection is complete and so I am perfectly just.

261

My dear children, as another night closes another day, you must ask yourselves a few questions.

What have I done for God today? What have I done that has offended God today? How can I avoid offending God tomorrow? Am I seeking God's will through prayer daily? How did I respond to the promptings of the Holy Spirit today? How have I used my time today? How have I treated other people today?

Reflect My children on the day you have just lived and struggle harder tomorrow to love Me more.

262

Go out into the day from your morning prayer
with a joy that is contagious.

263

Sanctification is the only preparation. Stay awake
for you know not when the Son of God is coming.

264

One by one.

265

Pride is ruling men's hearts instead of sorrow and
the love that is a consequence of that sorrow.
Return to confession and your ability to love Me
and all men will be renewed.

266

My dear children, you must build castles with your
interior lives for Me to live in. Ask yourself: Up
until now, what sort of house have I built within
me for God to live in? Then struggle to build a
great castle with all the elegance of a warm
summer's night.

267

Heaven is where love is the ruler and the slave, where love is the air and the sea, where love is the top and the bottom. Heaven My children, is love. Meditate on Heaven.

268

Can you feel My gentle hand guiding you today? No, then you need to abandon yourself again now.

269

Eternity is a long time.

270

All the wisdom on earth and in Heaven is found in children. I am Wisdom and you find Me in children. Now do you understand that if you are to love Me and share My wisdom with the world, then you need to make your mind, body, heart and soul a suitable vessel for My wisdom. My children you must be just that, children.

271

Mary attracts. Mary has an amazing ability to attract souls to a greater love of Me, the Lord your God.

272

Humility is so attractive.

273

In everything you do you must seek My Divine justice. The justice of the world is distorted by men's biases. My justice is perfect. Fight always for justice on earth.

274

Freedom is My gift to all people to enable them to show Me that they love Me.

275

Any wealth that is of the world is not worth having. Any wisdom that is of the world is not worth having.

276

Humility is the key to the Catholic faith and to Heaven.

277

All I ask of you is that you be a saint.

278

Look at the children, so innocent and pure, so humble. Look at the children, then be like them. For the mysteries of the Kingdom of Heaven are hidden from the proud and revealed to the littlest of all.

279

Take care of the poor My children. Take care of the poor, because it is there that lies the wealth. In the littlest of all, you will find the pure gold of love.

280

No one is more worthy of Heaven than a man who lays down his life for his friends or family. There are many out there who are doing this. There are many who are suffering the silent, hidden, martyrdom of service. Some do it for family; some do it for friends; some do it for strangers, and people they have never known. I tell you that if any man has a mind to belong in the Kingdom of Heaven he must renounce himself and serve his fellow man as he would be served himself.

281

Everything is secondary to your sanctification.

282

Open your heart. Be selfless.

283

Hearts melt because of the sweet love of prayer.

284

There is nothing more beautiful in a home than family prayer.

285

Here is a concrete resolution for you: try to help, or touch just one soul per day. If you do this you will leave a trail thick and wide of people loving Me, the Lord your God.

286

When you smell the scent of discouragement in your apostolate, say over and over in your mind to yourself: one by one, and then join the road to Heaven again with a loving trust in Me, your Heavenly Father.

287

Be humble and silent.

288

The secrets are: trust, perseverance and love.

289

The power of Eucharistic adoration is enormous.

290

Let nothing and no one distract you from doing
My will down to the last detail.

291

Pray and fast.

292

Love and be loved.

293

Interior life is the fountain from which living
waters will flow.

294

It is from the tabernacle that will come all the
strength and wisdom you need for all your
apostolic activity.

295

It is easier to create a whole new universe than to
change a man's heart; but prayer is all powerful.
Pray and trust.

296

Meditate on the passion and death of My Son
Jesus.

297
Give of yourself in everything for that is where your happiness lies.

298
Do not measure the success of your apostolic efforts on worldly scales, it is a spiritual matter.

299
Child, be a child of trust. As a child runs from danger towards the loving arms of his father, so should you. As a child shares a joyous occasion with his father, so should you.

300
The day is near when My Son will return to claim all that is His. Those of you who gather in humble obedience to Him in His Church on that day will share in the rewards of inheritance.

301
My children do not fret at the apparent darkness, just run to the light.

302
My child, those who love you for all the right reasons will love you ever so much more, the more they come to know you.

303

In a day your prayers and your actions, if done well out of love for Me, are enough to pour many, many graces upon a soul.

My child, each morning offer your prayers, works, joys and sufferings of the day to Me through the Immaculate Heart of Mary for a particular person or intention. This will allow you to love Me more.

304

The mission for each individual is clearly defined within each person's heart. Don't seek fancy techniques of obtaining holiness. Don't seek knowledge and theories as the source of holiness.

Holiness is merely a matter of embracing the moment lovingly and abandoning yourself trustingly to Me.

To be holy is to live in My love one moment at a time.

In your heart I have placed the answers to all your concerns. There is no need to fear, just pray and I will show you My will.

305

Go to the tabernacle My children, there you will find the precious body and blood of My Son truly present. Go to My Son, child, for He is the source of all love and all life.

Open your heart and your mind to contemplate on
the mystery of Christ's love for mankind. Each
drop of blood, each lash of the whip, each step
with the cross. Christ's blood has been shed for
you. Say it to yourself today and reflect upon it,
'Christ's blood has been shed for me.'

306

As the sun rises on a new day, turn your eyes to
Me. Reflect on the greatness of the day, then
reflect on the grandeur and magnanimity of your
God.

Look at the power of nature, the force of natural
sources, and then contemplate the strength of your
God. Contemplate My strength dear children,
because that is the strength you have behind you in
your work for Me.

Go then into each new day with a zeal for My
will, with a zeal to assist in the salvation of souls,
with a zeal to do nothing but My work at every
moment of the day.

307

I tell you, the examination of conscience, two or
three minutes per day, is the most effective and
powerful tool in keeping souls from becoming
lukewarm and for renewing zeal for the struggle.

308

The personal inadequacies of other people often challenge you to grow and change. Accept that each person is created as an individual and that every person who passes through your life does so for a particular reason.

309

Make your presence felt in the world: serve.

310

Take care of the details of each moment for this is the surest road to holiness.

311

Open your eyes My children to the beauty of a life of sanctity, not only because of the rewards that await you at the closing chapter of this life, but because of the wonderful and complete earthly happiness that is derived from living a selfless life in love with your God.

312

Purity My children, is the secret; watch only the things you should watch, see only the things you should see, look at only those things you should look at. Your eyes are the windows of your souls.

313

I have told you often that your happiness is central to Me making good use of you in My field. The harvest is great but the labourers are few. None the less, what blessing would sad labourers bring upon My field?

314

On the little, I bestow all My gifts; on the grateful, I bestow even more. Be grateful My children, for the many things that people in this world do for you, and be grateful to Me, the Lord your God, for all these gifts come to you from Me.

Don't be like the nine lepers who never returned!

315

Surrender and let Me form you child.

316

One resolution, one firm resolution. The rest will follow as a result of an exacting application of that one resolution.

317

Pray more My child.

318

Look into your hearts today My children. Tell Me, what do you find? Remove the division in your hearts and give your whole heart to Me; it is then that you will be able to love others to the best of your ability.

319

Nothing is more important than a belief, firm and fervent, that Jesus is My Son, the Son of God. If you believe this your actions will then start to reflect this belief. Reflect today on the fact that Jesus is My Son, the Son of God; reflect on the pain He suffered for you; reflect on the enormous love He has for you and has shown you.
Jesus is the Son of God. Do your lives reflect this belief?

320

From here (the tabernacle) shall come your strength and happiness. If only you would spend more time with My Son Jesus you would find peace of mind.

321

Peace, peace, they cry. Peace is another word so misunderstood in the world today. Violence can never lead to peace. Peace comes from within. Set peace within you and little by little you will set peace within the world.

322

Everyone seems to be in too much of a hurry. Slow down and see the beauty of a gentle but steady pace. Slow down and pray.

323

Holy men and women, that is what these times need.

324

Silence is beautiful. Come My children, spend time in silence with Me, the Lord your God. It is in silence that you come to know yourself and Me, your God. The world has been robbed of silence by modern technology and the push for material gain.

If you want and long for peace bring silence back into your lives, My children.

325

If only you knew the happiness that is to be found in doing My will, you would not hesitate for a moment.

Moment by moment decide for My will, and moment by moment live My will, abandon everything to Me, and 'now' will become your only concern.

326

Encourage people through your words and actions and win their hearts through your gentleness and serenity.

327

The virtue of poverty is not about not having things. It is about doing without things that you could have, in order to detach yourself from the world, so as to give your whole heart to Me, the Lord your God. Poverty is a virtue to be practised by all men and all women.

328

There are no coincidences, it is all Divine Providence and part of My plan.
My dear children see with eyes of faith and you will put depth and perspective into your lives.

329

When the whole world is against you, remember obedience and a clear conscience will be your greatest friends with Christ.

330

From adoration of the Blessed Sacrament come love, peace and vocations.

331

Your lives as Catholics must be lives of Christian community. You are brothers and sisters. You are children of light.

332

Nothing else is important until you have prayed My child. Pray, or else everything will fade and you will return to being your old self. And do you remember the worries and anxieties you held in your heart then?

Pray, for it is the only way you will maintain peace and joy in your heart and soul.

333

Of you I ask one thing, that you be a saint. Let this now intoxicate your heart, mind and soul. To be a saint!

334

Dedication to your vocation and a living love of God will come from living a good solid life of prayer.

335

Place your focus on one goal: the salvation of souls. Let this fill you with ambition and zeal to do My work. Reflect now in prayer on the value of one soul.

336

Look at yourself My child and examine your dispositions and the way you treat people. Examine the things you say and the things you do. Are you Christ-like? Are you trying really to be like Christ?

337

My dear child, today start to read the life of Christ in the four gospels and little by little you will grow to live like Him. Then when you speak with people they will say, 'this man or this woman is a person of prayer, a follower of Christ.'

338

Isn't it time you gave yourself to Me once and for all?

339

It is a well contemplated heart that is a pure heart. If you wish to have a pure heart then you must nurture this virtue through careful prayer and contemplation in silence. Silence is the key to having a pure heart.

340

Make your words and actions a song of prayer, the song of life.

341

My dear children, this year I would like for you to pick a friend. One friend, a person you know with whom you can build a stronger relationship and in time share with him, or her, the truth of your faith.

The faith My children, will spread through friendship. You must build friendships if you want the faith to spread.

342

My children, hold fast and seek lives of truth. Prepare the way for the Lord. With your lives of virtue, leave a trail of red carpet for My Son to walk in His second coming.

343

My children, do not be indifferent to venial sins. This will grow very quickly to a lack of sensitivity towards all sin and a general lukewarmness that leads a compromising and weak soul to hell.

344

Is it not true that among the men and women of the world are sprinkled a few that aim for the stars, who know and define ideals?

My child, in you I want for a person who struggles to achieve the ideal of a Christian life. Don't let the ideal be diluted during these times. Hold firm to the ideal now.

And what is that ideal? Sanctity of course. This is
the will of God, that you be a saint.

345

My child, breathe now, breathe. You have an
opportunity to take some deep breaths in your
spiritual life now. Make the most of this
opportunity.
Breathe deeply in prayer now and the air of prayer
will enkindle in you an even greater fire of My
love.

346

If only you would live the Mass, you would never
leave Me.

347

My child you must throw away the spirit of the
world and then you will answer My call lovingly.

348

Fortitude comes to a prayerful soul. The ability to
see God's will and the strength to do God's will,
this is fortitude.
I am the Lord your God, this vision and strength I
give to all who pray. Prayer increases the
abundance at which these gifts are given.
Come My children and pray and through the Holy
Spirit, I will administer to each of you the gift of
fortitude.

349

Saints are bred through mortification and prayer.
You must mortify your body so as to overcome it.
It is then that in your prayer you will achieve
greater union with Me, the Lord your God. This
union through prayer will in turn flow through
your life in the forms of acts of faith, hope and
charity. And a saint will be born and gradually
nurtured into eternity.

350

It is not that you are not doing enough My child,
but that you must make the most of all you do.

Those half-hearted conversations with people can
be transformed into fruitful apostolate.

The key to transforming these times into activities
that achieve greater glory for Me, the Lord your
God is, presence of God.

Pray more intensely, you will then be more aware
of My presence. And how does a prince act in the
presence of his father, the king?

351

You are not happy? Ask yourself why? Could it be
your diminishing interior life? Pray My child,
pray.

352

My child, if you pray everything else will fall into place.

353

My child, you see it is like this; you give the little that you can and I will add grace to it. And before you know it, together, but only by My grace, we will be moving mountains.

When you finally decide seriously to adopt a life of prayer and service you will begin to do great things. Things greater than you ever expected.

354

Trust in Me My child and then your hope will be full, your joy complete and your happiness of an eternal nature.

Come away from the hope of the world that always leaves you empty, disillusioned and lost. Place all your hope in the next life, in eternity, in your residence in Heaven.

355

My time with you child, is a time of rejuvenation. Come to prayer joyfully, for you will leave having gained the peace and serenity My Son Jesus came to bring all men. And with daily prayer this serenity will become unshakeable, for you are a child of God.

356

Do not dilute the ideal, let it remain ever firm in your mind: you were born to be a saint.

357

Sin My child, is the real enemy.

358

Beware occasions of sin.

359

Meditate on the gravity of sin.

360

My child, the road is long, but the rewards are great. Renew the struggle each day.

361

My child, in your heart you know.

362

Today is a new day at your feet; use it as though it were your last.

363

Peace of heart, peace of mind, peace of soul: the fruits of silence.

364

Time is plentiful if you just work hard.

365

Do you think I have a plan that does not allow enough time for you to do what I am asking?

366

What are you doing? Don't you know that I am your Father and you are My son and that the Kingdom of God is within you?

Pray My child, pray more.

367

Life is but a passing moment on this earth. Prepare yourselves My children to have eternal union with Me, your Heavenly Father.

368

Wisdom comes to those who ask with a humble heart. Impurity is a block to Wisdom. Guard your senses and your heart My children and you will grow to be wise sons and daughters of God.

369

No longer are you to concern yourself with those things of the world that your heart longs for and desires. Focus all your attention on Me and I will lead you in a love and a joy that all the things of the world could not bring you.

My child, concern yourself with eternity.

370

Beauty has always and will always live in love, and I am love. Allow Me to come and live in you. Let My love find a home in your heart and a path in your words and actions.

371

My child, act like a child of God and react when the tempter comes calling to you in time of weakness. React, don't dialogue with temptation, and call out to Me for strength in the dark night of temptation.

372

You ask Me to show you what I am asking of you but you never speak with Me about it.

373

My dear child, you cannot give what you don't have.

374

My love is like a gushing river running into your soul, when you come and spend time with Me in prayer.

375

Child, do you not see that many will ask things of you but I am asking much greater things of you?

376

Order My child. You know it is the answer. If you plan your days then you will be more efficient and more effective.

377

Persevere in prayer and all will be well.

378

Today My child, holds all you require. Love Me and today will be the day you focus on.

379

Open your heart now to the teachings of silence; they are greater and of more value than any worldly teachings.

380

Stand firm, say what needs to be said and must be said, but don't let things like this disrupt the peace and order in your soul.
Fear not child, I am with you and the sons of God will stand tall, long after everything else has fallen.

381

My child be peaceful, be calm, be serene. These are all the products of humility.

382

Do not be so worried. Let peace and joy reign in your heart still. Temptations will fade away, but the grace of God never.

I am your loving Father and I am with you always.

383

My dear children, today again I speak to you as My sons and daughters; the sons and daughters of God. Look at the world, look at the Church, what do you see?

So many of you would answer this question by telling Me all the things that are going wrong in the world and in the Church.

Today I would like to teach you about universal love which leads a person in possession of it, to adopt a positive, loving and forgiving outlook and advance the environments in which he works.

Love, a word confused and misunderstood in the modern world. I am the Lord your God, I am love; become like Me and then you will carry My love.

Forgiveness, I am the Lord your God and the author of forgiveness. Learn from Me, grow in Me, become like Me. Love and forgive everyone in your lives and then you will slowly begin to possess universal love.

384

Children, come to the water and drink of My Divine love. The love I have for you all flows to you in every moment of everyday, but you must open yourselves to My love.

This is achieved through prayer. Wandering through the wilderness of the world during these times you need to pray constantly. Invoke your mother Mary, her most chaste spouse, St. Joseph, the angels and the saints. Recognise that they are exalting in the true presence of Me, your Heavenly Father. Join your praise together with theirs. The songs of prayer and praise fill the whole earth but are you attentive to the rejoicing song that fills the ears of your soul? Sing praise to your God for He is good; Goodness is His name.

I am your Heavenly Father and more than ever I am calling you to the living waters of prayer and recollection.

385

Trust Me My child for I will take care of you. Don't cling to material possessions, or people, I will support you materially, emotionally and most importantly, spiritually.

386

My dear children, today again I call you to struggle in living the virtue of humility. Pride is the enemy of love and was the first sin of your parents, Adam and Eve. Pride saw Satan leaving Heaven and pride separates you from Me, your Heavenly Father.

Be humble in spiritual matters. Don't trust yourself too much. Keep silence. Silence is so necessary for you My sons and daughters, particularly in vain and useless conversations. Silence is a powerful tool in attaining the virtue of humility.

It is to the humble that I have always given My grace in so many forms.

387

Children, do you see how many distractions are in your lives? You are so used to living lives of distraction that when you do settle in a quiet, still peaceful environment you become easily agitated.

Distractions must be avoided. Solitude must be sought. Even if it is only for a few moments each day, your soul desires the solitude of silence, which brings rectitude of intention to your hearts, minds and souls.

388

How easily you are attracted to the things of this world My child. Can you not see that all this fades? Can you not see that eternity is the treasure?

389

The peace and order of your heart and your actions should reflect the life of Christ.

390

When you have virtue and peace, like a magnet you will attract people to Christ.

391

As the days go by you will come to see that your hunger to spend time with Me will grow more and more, if you nurture our friendship. This hunger you must respond to in two ways: firstly, by spending more time with Me, just the two of us together; and secondly, by trying to maintain constant conversation throughout the day. In every environment, in every situation, I am accompanying you as a friend. Speak with Me, as your friend I want to know.

392

Child, I want you to lead. I don't want for you to imitate anyone but Christ. I don't want you to compete with anyone. Success is not in this world but in the next.

I want you to discover that deep within you, is buried a unique and special person for whom I have a most glorious plan.

Child, I am your Heavenly Father.

393

I want for you to do something for Me very much in the middle of the world and so you must learn to love the world, for I created it. More than that, you must be cheerfully optimistic about the future of the world and of each individual.

Begin to see the Divine life within each person and this will relieve your heart of the weight from grudges that you hold against many people who have offended you in your work for Me. Don't mind the offence against you, pray and atone for their offence against Me.

394

Remember how Christ was treated. Can you expect any better? Disregard other people's expectations.

395

When the day comes for My Son to return, many will say, 'It is not He.' They won't recognise Him. Why? Because they will judge Him by the dictates of their hearts. His intentions are pure, theirs are not. Judge not, but know the Lord who saves.

396

By your ways and your works, men will know that you are of Me. Criticisms will come from those who see in you only a reflection of their own flaws. Don't worry, pray and move on.

397

The sower went out to sow. My child, go out and sow. Wherever you are, whoever you are with, you have an opportunity to sow. Don't waste opportunities. Life is a series of opportunities; your response to them is what determines your holiness.

398

Oh, you are so attached to the things of this world! My child, lift your eyes to greater things. Open your closed, cold, hard heart to My love and the beauty of life in Me.

Fading are the things of this world that your heart craves for. Show your heart something greater. Give your heart the consolation of constant prayer and the things of this world will fade into nothingness.

399

A new generation of priests, this is what is being prepared. Priests of purity. Priests of humility. Priests of devotion. Men who know the value of eternity. Men who are able to raise their eyes from the things of this world on to the greater things of the next world.

400

I am your loving Father, I hold you in the palm of My hand and I want for you peace, joy and happiness.

401

My child, smile, it is the joy of the soul.

402

Patience will see you become a light no one is able to put out.

403

As you wish to be treated, treat all men.

404

Could it be that you have been led to believe that unless you are suffering then you are not doing My will?

How many join you in this sad idea? Truth is happiness. Happiness is the perfume of God. Yes, My perfume is happiness and the Kingdom of God is within you.

405

Let those who walk in the glory of God, walk at God's pace.

406

Simplicity, where is it to be found in a world so complex? I'll tell you My dear child, in the hearts of the enlightened.

407

Counsel the moment for the truth it bears.

408

This world has very little to offer you, unless you are able to recognise the things of this world in the radiant light of the risen Christ.

409

Don't be anxious about family and friends. Let those who love God walk in faith, hope and love through these times of doubt. Let those who love God wait for Me to deliver each at the most appropriate time, to the fullness of life in the Spirit.

410

Happiness is the stone of great worth that I hang around each neck that I have anointed. Happiness is the great gift I offer you during these times by allowing you many choices. The happiness lies not in what you choose, but in how you approach what you choose. Choose carefully, for what you ask for may very well be what you receive.

411

Open yourself to My development of your many gifts and abilities. Open your life to the wonders and joys I am sending your way. Open your heart to the love I wish to fill you with. Great men are born every day and hidden in the fear of the unknown.

412

Little by little is the key to destroying the imperfect and restoring the ideal.

413
Learn to discipline yourself.

414
Every person who crosses your path comes bearing gifts.

415
Remember without Me, you can do nothing.

416
My child, an honest man is a good man. Tell no lies and live no lies and you will walk in the ways of Christ.

417
The Kingdom of God will be opened completely to those who approach Me with humility. It is the honesty of childlike humility that tears down all vanity and allows you to see, My child. Vanity distracts you from the real substance of life within Me.

418
It was always the proud that disputed My Son's teachings. Their hearts couldn't conceive honesty and so they judged Him by the dictates of their own hearts. Men judge by what they know.

419

Children live by what they know and what they see. Parents are the models of Christ in their lives. The words and actions of parents should allow children to be familiar with the gospel of Christ, long before they are able to read. Love is best conveyed without words.

420

I am your Heavenly Father and I long to gather all My children once again around the fire of My love and tell them the stories of faith, hope, courage, endurance and love that have carried the gospel message to the ends of the earth.

421

Wisdom grows in those that allow it to.

422

Now is a time when you must stop and reflect, and learn. The experiences that are filling your days, are speaking to you, if you will only be aware of the wisdom they wish to share with you. The fruits of living what you learn from your trials and experiences are growth in Christian virtue and unending joy.

423

The people who irritate you are there for a reason. They are there to teach you what annoys others in you.

424

My child do you intend to float always like a leaf in the wind? If this is the case it will only be a matter of time before someone treads on you and holds you down.

425

Silence is the great teacher; make it a good friend of yours.

426

While the consciousness and mentality of the world continues to remain largely at a superficial and material level, what is needed are men and women who are able to expand their horizons, widen their vision, to take in the realities of the spiritual realm.

427

A serene person is a prayerful well-contemplated person.

428

Love with detachment.

429
If you only knew what I am offering you, you would not hesitate for a moment.

430
Is it not time you started to really reflect upon and learn about the gospels?

431
Sustain the joy that fills your face with life by spending more time before the Blessed Sacrament.

432
All for the glory of God, so that all men may know the joy of Christ.

433
I have called you. Your life must change and some things must be left behind.

WHICH IS THE GREATEST OF THE COMMANDMENTS?

Jesus was teaching one day in the synagogue, to a large group of people, and from his position in the multitude a man asked Our Lord a question. He was a learned man, one of those doctors of the law who were no longer able to understand the teaching revealed to Moses because it had become so twisted and entangled in the ways of men. His question to Our Lord was, "Which is the greatest of the commandments?" Jesus opened His Divine lips slowly, with the calm assurance of somebody who knows what He is talking about and replied, "You shall love the Lord your God with your whole heart, your whole mind, and your whole soul. This is the first and the greatest of the commandments. And the second is like it, you shall love your neighbour as yourself. Upon these two rest the whole law and all the prophets."

And indeed upon these two rest each and every single one of our lives and for many hundreds of years, even thousands of years, men and women just like ourselves have been searching for practical ways to live these two commands in the middle of the world. The problem is very often, as human beings, when we are searching for something, we search in the wrong places.

There was a man who, as five o'clock came around each day, would rush out of the office and towards the bus stop. One day, after just making it to the bus stop on time, he jumped on the bus, bought a ticket and sat down. Three quarters of the way home he reached into his pocket for his house key only to find that in the hustle and bustle to get to the bus stop, he had lost his key.

He got off the bus at the next stop and ventured back into town retracing the steps towards his office in search of the lost key, but before long it became dark. Along the way he found a lamp post that shone some light on part of his journey and so he started searching for his lost key in the light that came from the lamp post. A couple of moments later, another man came along and asked, "Sir, have you lost something?" The first man replied, "Oh, yes, I've lost my house key." The second man, in his kindness, decided to assist this man in searching for his lost key and this went on for about fifteen minutes until the second man said to the first, "Sir, are you sure you dropped your key here?" And the first man replied, "Well, you know I'm not. In fact, I'm almost sure I lost it somewhere down near the corner but there is no light there."

As silly as it may seem very often this is how we live our lives. We know we have lost something, we know we are lacking something, we know we are searching for something, but we search for it in the light that comes from our limited past experiences.

And as most of us know, very often when the present moment presents a problem to us, the answers are not to be found in our past experiences, but rather it is at these times that God is calling to us; God is challenging us more than ever to step out of the light that comes from our limited past and to walk with Him down towards the corner in faith, and to see with the eyes of faith.

My name is Matthew Kelly. I am twenty-one years old and I come from Sydney, Australia. I was brought up there in Sydney and come from a large family. I have seven brothers and I am the fourth of eight boys. Up until part way through last year I was studying at university and more than anything else, I like to consider myself a fairly normal young person.

On the 7th of April last year, I was preparing to go to bed. It was about eleven thirty at night and I had been up since about five o'clock that morning. As I got into bed I reached for my walkman to listen to some music before I went to sleep and as I did, I had a strong feeling not to put my walkman on. I ignored the feeling, put the headphones on and as I turned on the music, the feeling continued to intensify. I then found myself getting out of bed and kneeling down beside my bed and doing the sign of the cross as though to pray. At that point of my life it was very unusual for me to be on my knees at any point of the day, never mind just before midnight. I knelt there somewhat confused in the darkness and the silence of the night for just a few moments and all in an instant I heard a voice speak to me, the voice I now know to be the voice of God, the Father, and I have been receiving what are termed interior locutions almost daily since.

I have had the pleasure of spending much of the last eighteen months of my life speaking with Bishops and priests, doctors and theologians, explaining how it happens, when it happens, where it happens and how often it happens. At the end of the day the most common conclusions drawn are two. Firstly, if this is happening, if God does speak to me and I don't assume that any or all of you believe that He does, then it is beyond science. We cannot do a scientific experiment and come up with the proof and say definitively, "yes, this is happening." And secondly, it is beyond the reasoning of the human mind. It is not something that we can reason through in our minds; it is not something we can put to a formula or an equation. And so for me to speak about how it happens, what it feels like, when it happens, where it happens and how often it happens, largely is fruitless.

A question very often asked however is, "Why would God do this?" or, "Why does God do this?" I don't suppose it is really for any of us here to say definitively why God would do anything, but let me tell you a story.

When I was seven years old and in grade one of primary school, I remember coming to the school gate week after week on a Friday afternoon and finding there at the gate three or four of my brothers who were very happy and excited because once again the school week had finished and the weekend had begun. But week after week on a Friday afternoon, far from coming to the school gate happy and excited, I was always sad and feeling low.

And I remember one particular Friday afternoon, the school bell rang and everybody raced out of class and ran toward the school gates. I gathered my things together slowly, packed my bag, tidied my desk and dragged my bag toward the school gate where I found four of my brothers once again, happy and excited. Only this week I was particularly sad. My mother came to pick us up and she took us and put us in the car with our school bags. I remember getting into the car and bursting into tears. My brothers looked at me wondering what had happened. Then my mother got into the car; she saw me crying and she said, "What's wrong?"

You see, on Fridays in grade one of primary school, we used to have our spelling test and I always failed. That made me sad. But I can still recall my mother taking me home and holding me in her arms and saying, "Everything is going to be all right." She continued, "We will practise your spelling and you will get better." She then asked, "How many did you get in your spelling test today?" I nervously replied, "six out of twenty." "That's fine" she said, "if you get seven next week I'll take you straight from school on Friday afternoon and buy you a big bar of chocolate."

I got seven, I got my bar of chocolate. Eight, nine, ten, twelve; more chocolate. Fourteen, sixteen, eighteen, nineteen, twenty; more chocolate. Until I had developed a love for chocolate, but I could also spell. And that is why God speaks to us, to encourage us.

God speaks to us to encourage us to walk along paths that we otherwise would be led to believe are impossible paths to walk. And God is speaking to us. Perhaps not very often in this very direct way, but through the people in our lives, through the people that cross through our lives, through the circumstances and events of our days God is speaking to us. Are we listening? Because when we begin to listen to the voice of God in our lives, we will begin to see that He is speaking to us to encourage us to walk in the ways of Christ.

It is not impossible to walk in the ways of Christ, but one thing is certain if we are to follow Christ, we need God's help, we need God's strength, we need God's encouragement, we need to listen to the voice of God in our lives.

The main theme that runs through the messages is that God calls every man and every woman without exception, regardless of age, occupation or vocation and from each of us He expects love, and He expects that love to be consistent and persevering. Now that is a lovely idea, and it is an idea that we have all heard many, many times before in our lives, but what God is saying is that now we have to try to take this idea out of the clouds and find practical ways to live it in the middle of the world wherever we find ourselves today, thus making it a reality.

If we look to the lives of the saints, it is very common for us to find that they loved God consistently and perseveringly. In fact more than finding this to be common in the lives of the saints, it is exactly this that made them saints. It is exactly this consistent and persevering love of God that made them holy men and women of God. We are each being called by God to the very same holiness. The problem is Holiness is one thing that is enormously misrepresented in the world. Some people think to be holy you have to run away from the world and find a cave to live in. Others think to be holy you have to be in a church on your knees praying for fifteen hours a day. Others still, believe that to be holy you have to walk around with a halo on; you're not allowed to smile or have any fun, or enjoy yourself at all. Too many people believe that holiness is like a gem lost in a haystack that nobody, or very few people, can find. These are all the very unnatural and unattractive ideas that the world proclaims about holiness when the reality is, there is nothing more attractive than holiness, there is nothing more attractive than virtue, there is nothing more attractive than Christ.

When Christ walked on the earth people wanted to be with Him. Whether He was speaking in the synagogue, walking down the street, or eating at a banquet, people wanted to be with Him. And so, when you and I begin to struggle to live the Christian life, we will begin to take on the attraction that Christ Himself had when He was on the earth. Why? Because it will no longer be you that lives, but Christ that lives in you.

However, if all of these ideas that the world is proclaiming about holiness are not really what it is all about, then we must ask ourselves, What is Holiness?

Holiness is an opportunity. Every person that comes into our lives, every circumstance and event of our lives, is an opportunity to be holy. Every moment of our lives presents an opportunity to grow closer to God. Our holiness is measured by how lovingly we respond to the people and events of our lives, how lovingly we grasp the moments of the day one by one for God.

Now, most of us recognise that we want to love God. The problem that we experience is that we are inconsistent in this love of God. We are inconsistent at grasping the moments of the day, one by one, for God. If we examine ourselves individually, the reason we will find for this inconsistency is that our lives of prayer carry traces of the very same inconsistency. When we feel like praying we pray, when we don't feel like praying, we don't pray. The problem is, if we link our love of God to our selfish feelings, indeed if our love of God is dictated by our selfish feelings, then obviously there is a contradiction, love being selfless.

It is for this reason that God calls us not only to pray, but to pray consistently. The more consistency we can bring to our lives of prayer, the more consistency we will bring to our ability to respond to God lovingly, by grasping the moments of the day one by one for Him. Each moment thus providing us with an opportunity to grow more like Christ, to grow closer to God, to become holier.

If we are to benefit from prayer in the way that God intends for us to benefit, then it is of paramount importance that we take some time to learn about prayer so that we can understand what we are trying to achieve. For too long people have viewed prayer as being a burden on our shoulders. Prayer is not designed to be a burden on our shoulders, but rather is designed to lift the burden from our shoulders.

We all share at least one thing in common here today and that is that we all yearn for happiness. Our yearning for happiness is a yearning for God. Unfortunately, for too long we have confused this yearning for God, this yearning for happiness, with a yearning for comfort, a yearning for money, for possessions, pleasure of the flesh and power. Our yearning for happiness is a yearning for God and only God can satisfy that yearning deep within us.

Yet still we search for our happiness in all the wrong places. How often we hear people say, "Well, when I have this new house, then I'll be happy."; or this much money or some new car. They search for their happiness outside of themselves, they search for their completion outside of themselves as if they were created incomplete. And how often we hear young people say that when they find the right guy or girl for them, the perfect partner in life, then they will be happy. Searching for their happiness outside of themselves, searching for their completion outside of themselves as if they were created incomplete.

Jesus said, "The Kingdom of God is within you." If we discover the Kingdom of God will we not also discover the happiness that we desire more than anything else? It is for this reason that God calls us to go within, to pray so that He can share His happiness with us. Too many people would have us believe that the perfume of God is pain and suffering. It is not. God's perfume is happiness and it is that happiness that He desires to share with each one of us in prayer.

Yet this happiness that we desire more than anything else in the whole world is only a by-product of our seeking, discovering and struggling to live the truth. But where might we search for the truth in a world that is so filled with falsehoods?

Let me tell you another little story. When God was creating the universe a few of the angels got together to discuss where God should hide the truth. One angel said, "I think God should hide the truth at the very summit of the highest mountain." Another said, "No, I think God should hide the truth in the very depths of the ocean." And a third angel, "Well, I think God should hide the truth on the furthest star." Then God came along and He said to the angels, "I will hide the truth in none of these places. I will hide the truth in the very depths of every man and every woman's heart. Therefore those that search humbly and sincerely and deserve to find it will find it very easily, and those that do not, will have to search the whole universe before they do."

How often though, do you and I find ourselves searching the whole universe? Jesus said, "the Kingdom of God is within you." If we discover the Kingdom of God, will we not also discover the truth that we seek? God is calling us to prayer, calling us to go within so that He can lead us.

The call however is a call to understand prayer. For ages past, men and women have continually misunderstood the practice of spiritual activity and as a result they have not been able to benefit from their practice.

Why is it that you take someone out to a football game and for three hours they are glued to the action; you cannot drag them away from the game, even for a hot dog. But if you bring them home and sit them down to pray or take them to Mass, in five minutes they are bored or asleep. Why? Because out at the football they understand the game, they know the tactics and techniques, they know the way the game flows, they know the players.

Until we bring a similar understanding to our practices of prayer and the Sacraments we will never experience the richness and beauty they were designed to achieve in our lives.

One of the first things we need to be aware of when we come to prayer is that as human beings, we have a body and a soul. It is also important that we understand that when we come to prayer, we are trying to align our hearts, minds and souls with God. It is this union with God that brings us the peace, joy and happiness that we all desire.

For this alignment to take place we need recollection. If we are to experience the benefits of prayer, it is of paramount importance that we take a few moments, even several minutes, before the practice of any spiritual activity and focus our attention on God and begin to direct our energies towards God and the things of the spirit. It is the process of recollection that leads us to slow down interiorly and exteriorly, allowing us to live the line from scripture, "Be still and know I am God." This recollection however requires a serious effort and the main effort required of us is to avoid and dismiss distractions from our mind. It has been my experience that this recollection is most effectively achieved in silence with my eyes closed.

Recollection cannot be rushed. When we come to pray, we need to be calm and set time aside so that we do not need to rush our prayer. So often we rush into and out of Mass without even thinking about what is happening, or say the rosary as if it is a race, or, we might have a couple of minutes to spare in the day, so we drop into a church and kneel in the back pew and say, "Listen up God, your servant is speaking. I want this, and this, and this, and this, and this and I asked for that last week, and why did you let this other thing happen, if you do that again I won't come to Mass on Sunday." Then rush straight out of the Church. Far from achieving any recollection, we become more distracted and flustered. Why are we always in a hurry when it comes to prayer? Because we are busy and we have all these other things that we need to do. Other things that will never be more important than our prayer.

Then from one group of people we hear, "I get nothing out of prayer," and from another, "You put nothing into prayer," but there are no answers in such an exchange. Rather, when we cry "I get nothing out of prayer," we must ask ourselves the question, "Where is my understanding of prayer lacking?" It is in answering this question that every person can improve his or her prayer life, and for most the first practical change to our practice of any spiritual activity will be to take time out to recollect ourselves. This will allow us to align our hearts, minds and souls a little more with God. This is union with God and the by-products of this union are the peace, joy and happiness that prayer and the Sacraments are designed to achieve in our lives.

There are many different devotions, many different practices of prayer. I would like to share with you today about only one. It is a practice of prayer that has had a profound effect on my life and one that has led me to an intimate friendship with Christ as a friend.

Jesus is your friend. How often when we have a problem or a decision to make we come to our friends and say to them, "Listen, I've got this problem..., this is the situation..., what do you think I should do?"

In one of the messages God the Father said, "All the answers are in the tabernacle." Jesus has all the answers, but when was the last time you sat before the tabernacle and said, "Listen, I've got this problem..., this is the situation..., what do You think I should do? Speak, Lord your servant is listening." When was the last time you gave Jesus a chance to place the answers in your heart?

In one of the messages God the Father said, "Go today and sit in front of a tabernacle and speak to My Son Jesus. Tell Him about all your worries and fears and He will remove all your anxieties. Tell Him about your plans for the day and the joys and problems you expect to encounter. Too many of you only tell Us of problems. Many beautiful things are happening, share them with Us in prayer. Speak to Us about everything that is happening in your lives. As your Friends, We want to know."

We all have worries and fears, we all have plans, we all expect to encounter different things in the day, we have joys, we have problems. These are the things we share with our friends. We share with our friends the things we have in common and the things that are important to us. We have everything in common with Christ, excepting sin; surely in that common ground we have the basis for a friendship.

We have to stop and reflect upon where our relationship with God is really at. Too many of us only tell God of problems. Do we only go to God when we have a problem? Too many of us only come to God when we want something. We've got to ask ourselves, "Do we only come to God when we want something?"

Let me tell you a little story. Once upon a time there was a young boy and Christmas was approaching and he wanted a bicycle, so he decided to write God a letter.

Sitting down to his desk he wrote, "Dear God, If You bring me a bicycle for Christmas I'll be a good boy for a whole year. Love Timmy." But looking at the letter he decided that this was too much and too hard and so he crumpled the page up and threw it in the garbage bin and began again, "Dear God, If you bring me a bicycle for Christmas I'll be a good boy for three months." Once again he decided that this would be too hard and so disposing of that page he began yet again, "Dear God, If you bring me a bicycle for Christmas I'll wash the dishes for three months. Love Timmy."

However, still he felt that this was too hard and so he crumpled up the page and threw it in the bin.

It was at this point that Timmy temporarily postponed his letter writing until he could come up with some more ideas. It was the following Sunday when his parents took him to Mass that the idea finally came to him.

While he was at Mass he noticed a beautiful statue of Mary, the Mother of God on the side altar. He had seen it many times before but it was on this Sunday that Our Lady's presence really struck him. Then when Mass was finished Timmy waited for everyone to leave, and when he was the only one left in the Church he went up to the side altar and taking the statue down he took it home and put it in his bedroom.

Then he sat down to write another letter to God, "Dear God, I've got Your Mother, bring me my bicycle. It wouldn't be much of a Christmas without Your Mother. Love Timmy."

We must ask ourselves, is our relationship with God like this? Are we always trying to bribe, blackmail, or strike a deal with God?

Jesus is calling us to a friendship and so to help us recognise the energies that we should be putting into our relationship with Jesus. Let us draw some parallels with our human relationships. Many of you are married, many of you have boyfriends or girlfriends. It is great to go out with your husband, wife, boyfriend or girlfriend to a play or a picnic, a dinner party or a movie, or with a group of your friends. It is also, however, very special to spend time one to one, just the two of you, with the one you love. In fact, it is this intimate time you spend one to one with the one you love, that makes the other times special, because it is during these times that you come to know each other a little more. In knowing each other a little more you are able to understand each other a little more.

The same is true of our relationship with God. We have time together in Mass, in prayer groups and in other ways with a group of people and our God. We need this time one to one with Jesus our friend in the tabernacle because just as in a human relationship, it is in this intimate time with God that we will increase our knowledge of Him and thus our understanding of Him.

It is clear that relationships break down because of a lack of understanding which stems from a lack of communication. If our relationship with God is broken down then we must question the level of communication and the way in which we communicate. At the end however, successful communication is the key to the success of any relationship and particularly our relationship with Jesus as a friend. Once we begin to establish this communication by setting time aside to spend with Jesus in the tabernacle, preferably every day, then we will begin to be aware of Jesus' presence at our side during the moments of the day. The friendly discussion that we began with Jesus before the tabernacle will flow into every moment of our days, making our lives one continuous journey towards Emmaus.

At every moment of our discussions here, we must remember that we are talking about love, we are talking about loving God. And, at this stage, let us recall how much energy we put into human love.

Although I am only twenty-one, I can certainly remember being in love once or twice in my life. I remember when I had a girlfriend, I would never walk past her house without dropping in to visit. Even if I was in a hurry I would just stop and knock on the door and say, "Hi, I'm in a hurry. Have a good day. I will talk to you later." Yet how often we have walked past a Church and far from not stopping in, we haven't even recognised that Jesus is present in the Church.

I can also recall that in times gone by when I had a girlfriend I would never let a day go by without calling her on the phone. Yet how often we have let days slip by without turning our hearts, minds and souls to God in prayer.

It is very clear in my memory also, that I never fell asleep on the phone to my girlfriend! You may laugh but can you relate to this scenario? You wake up and rush off into the day, it's a busy day and you get caught up in it and you return home late at night and think,

"Oh, I haven't done my prayer," but consoling yourself and relieving the weight from your conscience, you assure yourself that you will do it before you go to sleep. Then you lay on your bed and begin to say your prayers falling asleep before you finish praying. Are we talking about love? Are we talking about loving God? Because if we are talking about love, it is the same as falling asleep on the phone to your girlfriend.

Just a little earlier I heard you ask the question in your mind, "Do I have to do this prayer in front of the tabernacle? Can't God hear me wherever I am?" The answers to these questions are No and Yes, absolutely, BUT, are we talking about love?

My memory also serves me well enough to tell you of one or two things I learnt about teenage love, in my limited experience of it. I learnt that if you are really interested in a girl, you have to go to the parties that she goes to, otherwise you have not a chance of meeting her, never mind getting to know her. We have to go to where Jesus is at. Jesus is waiting for us in the tabernacles of our Churches.

Another thing that I learnt was that if you were really, really interested and you are serious about getting to know her, then you don't take her out to the big parties or the nightclubs, you take her down to one of those nice coffee shops and buy her a cappuccino, some chocolate mudcake and you talk to her. You get to know her in an environment that lends itself to that.

We need to spend time with Jesus in an environment where we can get to know Him better.

It is time we recognised how much energy we put into human love and started to put similar, if not greater energies into our love of God.

We need to set time aside to pray. All too often we find ourselves putting our prayer off until a more convenient time. We wake up in the morning and something inside us tells us to pray but there are so many pressing matters, we convince ourselves that it will be more beneficial to do it at another time. So we say to God, "Not now God, later." The morning passes and another opportunity arises but once again we find ourselves coming up with reasons to delay it even further and again we say, "Not now God, later." This set of circumstances then gathers momentum and are repeated over and over, day in and day out.

Patiently God is sitting up in Heaven and this is what a transcript of our conversation with God looks like, "Not now God, later. Not now God, later. Not now God, later. Not now God, later. Not now God, later. Not now God, later. Not now God, later. Not now God later...". Very monotonous isn't it?

We need to set time aside to pray and it is preferable if that time can be the same time every day because by anchoring our days to this time of prayer, we will begin to deal with the challenges of our days more creatively and cheerfully with a peacefulness that is not affected by the fluctuating emotions or circumstances in our life.

Let me ask you, do we appreciate Jesus in our tabernacles? I dare say we do not and I would like now to tell you a story to explain, but a story that I hope will help us all to appreciate the Blessed Sacrament a little more today and in the future.

While I was in America recently, I was reading a letter from a priest. The content of his letter concerned his experiences as a lay missionary in China forty years ago. He then went on to say that two years ago he, incognito, returned to China for a brief visit. Because of the problems existing there, nobody in China knew that he was a priest.

On the second night of his visit, he was awoken in the middle of the night by the noise of people moving around the house. A little scared, he got up out of bed and went to his door. Opening his door he grabbed one of the men living in the house and said to him, "What is going on?" The Chinese man replied, "We're going to the wall." He inquired further, "What is the wall?" The Chinese man replied, "Come with us and we will show you."

There were many people living in the house and while none of them knew that he was a priest, they knew that he could be trusted. Not satisfied with the answers he had received, he went downstairs and found one of the older women whom he had known from forty years earlier and asked her, "What's going on? Where are you all going?" She gently replied, "We're going to the wall." He persisted, "What is the wall?" She replied with the same gentleness, "Come with us and we will show you."

He got dressed and ventured out into the night with this group of people walking for miles and then they were joined by two other groups until they numbered almost one hundred and twenty. They then came to a forest and as they began to walk into the forest, he noticed that some of the male members of the group were climbing up trees.

Before long they came to a clearing in the forest and there in the middle of the clearing was a small half built wall from an old derelict building. The old woman turned to him and smiled with all the love she had in her heart. At this stage he looked up to notice that there was a circle of men from their group surrounding the clearing in the trees above. The group at this stage was walking into the clearing towards the wall and as they came close they fell down on their knees before the wall.

Moments later, one man got up and walked towards the wall, then reaching forward with one hand he took one brick out of the wall and behind that brick was reserved the Blessed Sacrament. They adored the Blessed Sacrament for one hour in silent prayer. Then the same man got up and approaching the wall, he replaced the single brick. The men came down from the trees and they went home.

The next day he told them that he was a priest and he in turn was told that they had not had Mass there in ten years and that the Host had been in that wall for ten years. Two or three times a week they would go to the wall in the middle of the night, risking their lives to spend an hour with Jesus their greatest friend.

The priest said Mass at the wall the next night and replaced the Host.

Do we appreciate Jesus in our tabernacles? If discovered that evening, those one hundred and twenty people would have been imprisoned and quite possibly killed. You and I, we can come to Jesus freely whenever it be our desire; we don't have to risk our lives. Jesus is our greatest friend. He has all the answers and He has been waiting for us in the Blessed Sacrament for nearly two thousand years. For how much longer will you continue to put Him off? For how much longer will you continue to ignore such a great friend?

One important aspect of this time of prayer is silence, because it is in silence that we discover ourselves and in silent prayer that we discover our God. We discover ourselves and the weaknesses and limitations that we have, we discover God in His greatness, and we feel the challenge and inspiration to grow and become more like our God.

If we want to be wise, silence must become one of our great friends. God bestows His Wisdom upon men and women in the classroom of silence. If you want to be wise, get to know yourself in the classroom of silence with God in prayer. After knowledge of God, there is no greater practical wisdom than knowledge of self. It is at this point that we have stumbled across the reason why so many abandon prayer, because when they come to pray they grow in their knowledge of God, they grow in their knowledge of self, but are unable to respond to Christ's challenge to change. So, may God grant us wisdom enough to pray and strength enough to live what we discover in prayer.

We read in the gospels of Jesus' meeting with many individuals. Meetings of love, meetings of mercy, meetings of compassion and forgiveness, but always meeting with a message. Christ's message to every man and every woman He encountered in these meetings was CHANGE, and His message is the same to us today. Jesus wants us to change, but the reality is that we don't want to change. We're happy doing what we are doing, where we are doing it, when we are doing it and we say to God, "Listen, Lord, I've got these plans. They are good plans, there is nothing wrong with them, they don't hurt anybody and they are not sinful." God's response to this however, is, "That's all fine, but abandon your plans to Me because I have something else, something greater planned for you." It is this abandonment that we all have so much trouble with.

Let me tell you a little story about three trees and their plans and ambitions.

In the depths of the forest one day, there were three trees standing side by side and this day they got to talking. One of the trees started the conversation voicing his ambitions saying, "When I get cut down I want to be a cradle to hold a baby, because cradles are the centre of attention and affection for everybody within a household." With this, the second tree spoke up in a loud voice saying, "No, when I get cut down I'd like to be a sailing yacht to carry the rich and famous people of the world across the harbours of the world." A few moments passed and then finally the third tree spoke up quietly saying, "You know, if I am ever cut down I'd like to be a signpost to direct people along the right path. To show people back to the right path when they are lost and astray."

Time went by and before long the three trees were cut down and taken off to the mill for processing. And soon after that, a man came along and took the first tree away. The first tree had expressed a desire to be a cradle and there was nothing wrong with that, but there was something else planned. The man took the tree away and turned it into a dirty old stable to house sheep and cattle and donkeys. Then another man came to the mill for the second tree. This tree wanted to be a sailing yacht, there was nothing wrong with that, but there was something else planned. The tree was taken away and turned into a filthy old fishing boat that was constantly inhabited by the dirty smell of dead fish. And before too long the third tree was also taken from the mill. The third tree wanted to be a sign post, truly a noble plan for a humble tree, but there was another plan. This third tree was taken away by a centurion and made into a cross for crucifying criminals.

Now it would seem that the three trees, their plans and ambitions had disappeared, faded into nothingness. It would seem that they had failed in the achievement of the plans and ambitions.

However, it was not long until one winter's night a young man came along. It was cold, he had his wife with him and they had nowhere to stay. So they made that stable their home for the night. That mother was Mary and she gave birth to Jesus, our Saviour, that night in the stable. The stable, the first tree, had wanted to be a cradle so that it could hold a baby and be the centre of attention and affection. It thought to do this, it had to be a cradle. It didn't, it needed to be a stable, because it was as a stable that it became the centre of attention and affection, not only for the people of those times, but for the people of all times. Even to this day that stable is still the centre of attention and affection in our homes and Churches at Christmas.

The child grew up, He was the Christ and He walked through the streets of the world proclaiming the Good News of the Kingdom of Heaven. The second tree, the fishing boat, got to carry the richest, the most famous person ever to walk the face of the earth across the harbours of the world. The second tree had believed that to carry important people it would have to be a sailing yacht. It was wrong. It needed to be a fishing boat. And as a fishing boat it became the platform from which our Saviour levelled His messages not only to the people of that time but to the people of all times.

But, He was just a young man and He spoke His message far too clearly and uncompromisingly. Where there was darkness He was trying to shine a light, while other people were guarding the light switch. He challenged the people both above Him and below Him to CHANGE in a way that was far too direct for their liking. So as always, when people don't like the message, they kill the messenger. In that light they dragged Him outside the gates of the city and on that cross, the third tree, they crucified Him.

The third tree had wanted to be a signpost and indeed it became the greatest signpost of all times. The cross, the signpost that leads us along the right path. The cross, the signpost that leads us back to the right path when we are lost and astray.

The three trees had plans and ambitions just as you and I have plans and ambitions. They could not however, have foreseen what was in store for them;

they couldn't have planned what was in store for them. Neither can you nor I plan or foresee what God has in store for us, if only we will abandon ourselves into His loving arms. And it is this abandonment that causes us to stumble so often. It is the prospect of needing to abandon ourselves to God that scares some people so much that, rather than do this, they abandon God.

Our recognition of the need for each of us to abandon ourselves to God must lead us to seek out practical ways of achieving this abandonment. God is calling us to prayer. By praying a little more we will get to know Him a little more; by knowing Him a little more we will be prepared to trust Him a little more; and in trusting Him a little more we will be able to abandon ourselves a little more to Him. Pray, know, trust, abandon. Pray, know, trust, abandon.

The first part of the quote we started with was, "You shall love the Lord your God with your whole heart, your whole mind, and your whole soul." We have looked at practical ways of struggling to live this command and primarily we have discovered that the more consistency we can bring into our life of prayer, the more consistency we will bring to our ability to respond to God in the other moments of the day. It is in this moment by moment response to God that our holiness lies.

The second part of Our Lord's reply was, "Love your neighbour as yourself."

When we live our faith, when we love God, a few things are going to happen. Firstly, we are going to become happier people and as a result of this happiness we are going to have more friends. Why? Because people like to be around people who are happy because they, in turn, make them happy. Another thing that is going to happen when we love God, when we live our faith, we are going to become one of those people that everybody admires, because they are able to keep a level head in the midst of difficulties or trials and just concentrate on effecting what they can effect in any given moment of time. And thirdly, when we live our faith, when we love God, our love of God is going to automatically manifest itself in a love for the people around us.

Then, when you have that happiness, that level headedness, and that love for the people around you, people are going to ask, 'What makes you different? Who or what inspires you to live the life you live?' People will begin to notice that you are different and they will be attracted and they will want what you have. Why? Because there is nothing more attractive than holiness. It is at this point that we have the greatest opportunity to spread the faith, when others can see that we have something worth having; but you cannot give what you do not have.

This is why God is calling us to turn on the tap of our spiritual lives, not to full blast, just to a steady, consistent, persevering drip; a dripping tap. If you put a bucket under a dripping tap eventually the bucket will fill and once it is full, it has to overflow; the water has nowhere else to go.

The tap is your spiritual life. The drops of water are the peace, joy and happiness that flow from prayer. The bucket is your heart, your soul.

Drop by drop through prayer you are filled with peace, joy, love and happiness and once your heart and soul are full, they have to overflow. There is nowhere else for them to go, and so, everywhere you go, every person you are with, begins to be filled with these gifts through your words, action and even by your mere presence. When we love God the change necessary in society and the conversion of the people around us will not have to be premeditated, it will be natural.

On a community level, when we have this happiness, level headedness and love for the people around us, people will come; people will most definitely come. There will be no spare seats in our Churches on Sundays; our priests will have to say more Masses and hear confessions for longer; we will have more Churches; we will have more priests; our seminaries will begin to fill again; and vocations will begin to flow again to the religious states of life. Why? Because all of these things are the fruits of love. If there are not enough of these things, then there is not enough love and that is a matter for each of us individually as part of the one body of Christ. As sad as it may sound, the thing that would seem to be lacking most in the Church during these times is the love of Christ. Have we lost it? Or just misplaced it? Because it is clear that when we find it, people will come.

Let us now go up into the upper room with Jesus and the disciples at the last supper. Imagine you are there and Jesus turns to His disciples and says, "I give you a new commandment, love one another as I have loved you. It is by this that all men will know that you are My disciples."

Jesus also said in Holy Scripture, "Learn from Me for I am gentle and humble of heart," but He didn't say to His disciples that night, "All men will know that you are My disciples because you are gentle and humble of heart." Jesus was the purest ever to walk on the face of the earth, but He didn't say to His disciples that night, "All men will know that you are My disciples by the purity and chastity you live." Jesus owned nothing, He was completely detached from everything in this world, but He didn't say to His disciples, "All men will know that you are My disciples because you are not attached to the things of this world." No, He said, "Love one another ... it is by this that all men will know that you are My disciples."

It is our love for one another that identifies us as Christian. Have we lost our identity as Christians in the middle of the world during these times? Do you need to rediscover your identity as a Christian?

When we have this love, the gentleness, humility, purity, detachment will all flow from this love. This love however, is gained by a change within. Personal holiness is the beginning and the answer to everything.

In the distant past they used to use stories to convey messages of profound meaning. Throughout the ages, regardless of creed, colour, race, tradition or religion, men and women have found stories to be the most powerful way to convey any message. I'd like to share another story with you now that sums up very clearly and simply the starting point that God is giving each and every single one of us.

There was a very successful businessman one day, who had a very large company, but business was not too good and his company was in a lot of trouble. From all external signs it appeared that his company was going to go down and his competitors were ready to pounce on his market share.

None the less this man had a plan that he knew, without a doubt, would revive his company.

It was Saturday morning and he was preparing a speech to give at his company's annual dinner for staff that evening. He wanted to show them the first part of the plan, but more than that he wanted to emphasize to them, that if his plan was to be successfully and speedily executed it was dependant on the individual response of each one of his employees.

He was writing his speech and his wife had to go out shopping. Within ten minutes of his wife being gone there was a knock on the study door, and there appeared his young seven year old son and exclaimed, "Dad, I'm bored."

And so the father half tried to amuse the child by playing a game with him whilst half trying to write and finish his speech at the same time. This went on for nearly two hours until he worked out that, unless he could find some other way to amuse his son, he was not going to finish his speech in time.

So he picked up a magazine, and flicked through the magazine until he found a large brightly coloured map of the world and he tore the page out and ripped it into many pieces. Knowing his son was already influenced by his business initiative, the father threw the pieces all over the living room floor, with the words, "Son, if you can put the map of the world back together, I will give you a dollar."

The child rushed to the task and the father returned to his study believing that he had just bought himself two, maybe three hours to do his speech because the father also knew that his seven year old son had no idea what the map of the world looked like. But within ten minutes, there was a knock on the study door, and there appeared his son smiling with the completed puzzle.

The father in amazement said to the child, "Son, how did you finish it so quickly?"

The child smiled larger than ever and said, "Well, I had no idea what the map of the world looked like Dad, but there was a picture of a man on the back."

The child then continued saying, "I put a piece of paper down, I put the picture of a man together, I put another piece of paper on top and turned them both over. I took the top piece of paper off and there was the world, complete and in order."

The father stood there in silence and amazement, and the boy continued once more.

"Dad, I figured, if I got the man right, the world would be right."

And this is what God is saying to you and I today. Look at yourself and make a change, because everything good and everything bad in this world comes from an individual. It is the influences and effect of individuals' words and actions, men and women just like ourselves, that have formed the world to be the place it is today.

The problem is, we got the man wrong and the world continues to go wrong. We get the man wrong, the man continues to worry about what everyone else is doing wrong and the world continues to go wrong. We get the man wrong, the man continues to worry about everything that is going wrong that he cannot effect and the world continues to go wrong.

It is when individuals like you and I stop and take time to reflect and begin to effect what we can effect, that we will begin to have an effect. It seems all very simple because it is. It is the influences and effects of your words and actions that form the world of tomorrow. When you start to channel your words and actions in a positive Christian way, it is then that the world will begin to resemble a little more, the place God created it to be. If we get the man right, it is only a logical consequence that we will get the world right.

Jesus was teaching one day in the synagogue to a large group of people, and from his position in the multitude a man asked Our Lord a question. He was learned man, one of those doctors of the law who were no longer able to understand the teaching revealed to Moses because it had become so twisted and entangled in the ways of men. His question to Our Lord was, "Which is the greatest of the commandments?" Jesus opened His Divine lips slowly, with the calm assurance of somebody who knows what He is talking about and replied, "You shall love the Lord your God with your whole heart, your whole mind and your whole soul. This is the greatest of the commandments. And the second is like it, you shall love your neighbour as yourself. Upon these two rest the whole law and all the prophets."

And indeed upon these two rest each and every one of our lives. So, as we struggle to live these two commands in the middle of the world, we must allow ourselves to be encouraged by God through prayer. If we are to resist the ever present pressures to dilute the Christian ideal that surround us at every level of society and in almost every environment, one thing is certain and that is that we need God's help, we need God's strength, we need God's encouragement. We need to come before Him, humble in prayer and allow Him to transform our lives. And as we struggle to walk in the ways of Christ, we need to encourage those that are at our side, because it is absolutely clear that Jesus wants to touch every person on this earth; Jesus wants to extend the hand of love and friendship to every person. The problem is very often the only hand Jesus has to extend is the one that is attached to the end of your arm.

Now as we finish tonight and at each moment on our journey towards God, let us keep one thought forever on our hearts and in our minds, and that is, for those that love God there is only victory, and victory for eternity.